# Grandpa's Scrapbook

by Peggy Bresnick Kendler
illustrated by Pamela M. Anzalotti

PEARSON

Scott
Foresman

Editorial Offices: Glenview, Illinois • Parsippany, New Jersey • New York, New York
Sales Offices: Needham, Massachusetts • Duluth, Georgia • Glenview, Illinois
Coppell, Texas • Ontario, California • Mesa, Arizona

"Grandpa, tell us a story!" Elizabeth said to her grandfather. Elizabeth and her brother Jesse were visiting their grandfather.

"Yes, Grandpa! Please tell us a story!" Jesse said.

"I'll do better than that," their grandfather said. "I'll show you a story!"

Elizabeth and Jesse were lucky. Their grandfather was Mark Twain. He was one of America's favorite writers.

Not only did he write the best stories, but he told the best stories too. They were all about his childhood in his homeland of Missouri.

"How are you going to show us a story, Grandpa?" Jesse asked.

Grandpa pulled a big, worn book out of a tall bookcase. "This is my special scrapbook. It has pictures of the places I loved when I was your age. It's a book full of wonderful adventures."

Jesse and Elizabeth sat on the floor next to their grandfather. His scrapbook was set out in front of them. Grandpa was a tall man. Even when they were all sitting down, he was towering over them.

"Let's begin," Grandpa said. The children sat as quietly as sculptures.

"My hometown is Hannibal, Missouri," Grandpa said. "There is a big river there. It is called the Mississippi River, and it is about a mile wide!" Twain used some of his own childhood adventures in his famous books about Tom Sawyer and Huckleberry Finn.

Grandpa showed them a picture of three boys playing by the river. "That's me and my friends," Grandpa said. "We always pretended we were pirates! We longed for adventure."

"That river amazed me. We swam in it all summer," Grandpa said. "In winter, we would sneak out of our houses late at night to go skating!"

Grandpa showed the children a picture of himself at home in bed. "This is me after I fell through some thin ice into the river," Grandpa said. "I was sick in bed for three weeks."

"We loved to explore the caves along the river," Grandpa said.

He pointed to a drawing of a girl. "This is Laura Hawkins. We bewildered her, but she still sometimes went on adventures with us in the caves outside of town and on the river," he said.

In his books about Hannibal, Laura Hawkins was the model for one of the main characters, Becky Thatcher.

Jesse and Elizabeth looked up at Grandpa in awe. "Show us more!" said Elizabeth. She tried to still herself so she could listen.

"This part of the scrapbook is full of pictures from later in my life," Grandpa said. "It's from the time when I was a steamboat pilot."

"A steamboat pilot? You drove a steamboat, Grandpa?" Jesse asked.

"Yes, Jesse. I couldn't imagine anything more fun than to drive a steamboat." Grandpa pointed to a steamboat ticket he had pasted on the page.

"When I was 22 years old, I became a cub pilot on Mississippi River steamboats," Grandpa said. "A cub is someone who is just learning. I trained for 18 months."

Grandpa showed the children a picture of himself as a young steamboat pilot. "I got my license in 1859!" Grandpa said proudly.

"Where did you go?" Jesse asked.

Grandpa pointed to pictures in the scrapbook. "I went up and down the Mississippi River. I saw New Orleans, Louisiana, and St. Louis, Missouri, over the next three years. We hauled cotton, tobacco, and other goods to be sold. We carried travelers from port to port. Steamboats were very important to life on both sides of the Mississippi River."

St. Louis, Missouri

Grandpa closed the scrapbook and smiled at the children. "That's enough for today," he said.

"No, Grandpa!" Elizabeth and Jesse said at the same time. "Show us some more stories!"

Just then, the children's parents came into the house. "I know what *that* means," their mother said, pointing to the big scrapbook. "When I was young, your grandpa used to show me stories too."

"Next time," said the children's father, "I want to be here to see them too!"

# Samuel Clemens

Mark Twain was born Samuel Langhorne Clemens in 1835. Mark Twain was Samuel's pen name. A pen name is not a real name. It's a name people use when writing books. The name "Mark Twain" comes from a riverboat term meaning two fathoms. A fathom is a unit of measure equal to six feet. The term is used most often to talk about the depth of water. Can you think of why Clemens chose this for his pen name?

Mark Twain was one of America's best-known writers. He wrote many books for children and adults. In addition to writing books and working as a riverboat pilot, Twain held many other jobs. He worked in print shops and wrote for newspapers. He prospected for gold and traveled to foreign countries. He married Olivia Langdon in 1876.